Watch It Grow
Pumpkin

Barrie Watts

W
FRANKLIN WATTS
LONDON • SYDNEY

First published in 2002 by Franklin Watts
96 Leonard Street, London EC2A 4XD

Franklin Watts Australia
56 O'Riordan Street, Alexandria, NSW 2015

Editor: Adrian Cole
Art director: Jonathan Hair
Photographer: Barrie Watts
Illustrator: David Burroughs
Consultant: Beverley Mathias, REACH

A CIP catalogue record for this book
is available from the British Library

ISBN 0 7496 4433 8

Dewey Classification 635

Printed in Hong Kong, China

How to use this book
Watch It Grow has been specially designed to cater for a range of reading and learning abilities. Initially children may just follow the pictures. Ask them to describe in their own words what they see. Other children will enjoy reading the single sentence in large type, in conjunction with the pictures. This single sentence is then expanded in the main text. More adept readers will be able to follow the text and pictures by themselves through to the conclusion of the life cycle.

Contents

Pumpkins come from seeds.

This pumpkin seed is the size of a grape. It came from the middle of a pumpkin fruit that weighed over 9 kilograms. The seed was dried and stored during the winter.

In the spring, when the weather is warm, the seed is planted. It will grow into a new pumpkin plant. Inside it are a root, a shoot and **seed leaves** that the plant needs to start to grow.

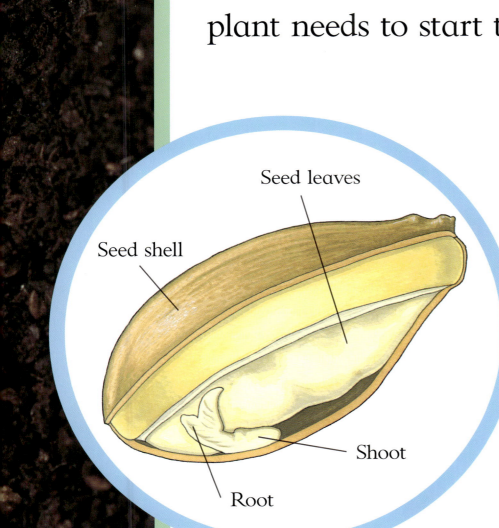

Seed leaves

Seed shell

Shoot

Root

The seed gets wet.

When the soil around the seed gets wet, the shell of the seed becomes soft. Using energy from food stored inside the shell, the seed pushes out tiny roots.

The roots collect water from the soil. After three days the stem and leaves sprout from the seed. They start to grow up towards the surface of the soil.

The seed leaves grow.

The first leaves that grow on the stem are called **seed leaves**.
The leaves are folded up so they do not get damaged as they push up towards the surface of the soil.

When the seed leaves reach the surface they unfold. They use sunlight to make food. Later, the seedling will grow bigger leaves.

The proper leaves grow.

After one week, the proper leaves start to grow. They make even more food which is carried through **veins** in the leaf.

Each new leaf that grows on the pumpkin plant is bigger than the one before. The largest leaves will measure 40 centimetres across. The **seed leaves** are no longer needed. They turn yellow and die.

The roots grow deeper.

The pumpkin plant sends out thousands of roots into the soil. The roots are covered with tiny hairs.

The tiny hairs pass water from the soil back through the roots to the plant. As the pumpkin plant gets bigger it needs lots of water.

The flower buds grow.

After four weeks, buds begin to appear on the stem of the pumpkin plant. Growing inside each bud is a large yellow flower.

The longer the stem grows, the more flowers the pumpkin plant will have. The flowers will open at different times. This stops them all being destroyed if the weather is bad.

A flower opens.

After eight weeks, the yellow flower opens and its large petals unfold. Flowers are either male or female. A male flower is small. A female flower is big and has a tiny fruit growing behind the petals.

Pollen in the male flower must pass to the female flower before the fruit can grow any bigger.

Bees visit the flowers.

Pumpkin flowers open in the morning. Bees are attracted to them by the sweet-smelling **nectar**.

When a bee visits a male flower, **pollen** gets stuck to its body. Then, as the bee collects **nectar** from a female flower, the pollen is brushed off on to the **stigma** in the middle of the flower. This **fertilises** the female flower.

Pumpkin flowers are only open for one day. They close in the evening and die.

The pumpkin fruit changes.

After the female flower is **fertilised,** the small fruit gets bigger. The petals die. The skin of the fruit changes colour and it becomes shiny and begins to harden.

The pumpkin fruit's shiny, tough skin protects it from **pests**.

If the flower is not **fertilised** the fruit will dry up and fall off the plant.

The pumpkin fruit gets bigger.

If the weather is warm and sunny, and the roots find plenty of water, the pumpkin fruit will grow quickly. It takes three months from when it was planted as a seed for the pumpkin plant to grow large fruit.

The fruit of a pumpkin plant can grow up to 5 centimetres a day. It becomes too heavy for the stem to support and grows downward until it rests on the soil.

Seeds grow inside the fruit.

The fruit begins to grow its own seeds. At first they are very small and are joined to the fruit by thin threads. These pass water and food to the seeds so that the seeds can grow bigger.

Each fruit can have up to 200 seeds inside it. They are protected by the fruit's soft flesh and tough skin.

The pumpkin fruit is fully grown.

After six months, the pumpkin fruit has grown to its full size. It can be as big as a basketball. About 80 per cent of the pumpkin is water. The hard skin stops the fruit drying out.

The pumpkin is **harvested**
in the early autumn.
As the weather gets colder,
the rest of the plant turns
yellow and dies.

Pumpkin fruit has many uses.

If the pumpkin is stored in a cool, dry place, it will keep for months without going rotten. Its soft, juicy insides can be made into pies and cakes.

At Halloween, the hollowed out pumpkin can be used to make a scary face.

The seeds can be dried and planted the following spring.

Word bank

Fertilised, Fertilises - A female flower is fertilised when pollen from a male flower comes into contact with the female stigma. This happens when insects move from one flower to another looking for nectar. Only a fertilised flower will grow large fruit and seeds.

Harvested - When fully grown crops are collected by people from fields or gardens.

Nectar - A sweet, sugary liquid that attracts bees and other insects to flowers. Bees make honey from nectar.

Pests - In this example, any creature that damages a crop. Snails are a pumpkin's main pest.

Pollen - A fine yellow powder that is produced by male flowers.

Seed leaves - The first leaves that grow on a plant. When proper leaves begin to grow, seed leaves turn yellow and die.

Stigma - The part of a female flower which receives pollen from a male flower. When this happens the flower is fertilised and produces fruit.

Veins - The tiny tubes in a leaf that carry food to the main stem of the plant.

Life cycle

Three days after being planted, the pumpkin seed has sprouted roots and the stem starts to grow.

After six months the fruit is fully grown. Next spring, the seeds inside can be planted to make more pumpkins.

The seed leaves push to the surface and unfold.

Seeds grow inside the fruit.

After one week, the proper leaves grow.

After three months, the fertilised flower produces large fruit.

After four weeks, flower buds start to appear on the plant stem.

After eight weeks, the flower bud opens and attracts insects.

Index